Germinal G. Van

EQUAL UNDER THE LAW

A Reflection On Amendment XIV and the Concept of Citizenship

A Reflection on Amendment XIV

EQUAL UNDER THE LAW

A Reflection on Amendment XIV

EQUAL UNDER THE LAW

Table of Contents

About the Author..P.7
Acknowledgements..P.11
Author's Note..P.15
General Introduction...P.19

PART I:
The Historical Analysis of Amendment XIV..P.23

Introductory Argument.......................................P.25

Chapter I:
The Creation of Amendment XIII........................P.29

Chapter II: The Fourteenth Amendment and its Ratification P.37

Conclusive Argument..P.46

PART II:
The Legal Analysis of Amendment XIV..P.51

Introductory Argument..................................... P.53

Chapter III:
The Citizenship Clause.....................................P.55

Chapter IV:
The Privileges or Immunities Clause................P.67

Chapter V:
The Due Process Clause..................................P.77

Chapter VI:
The Equal Protection Clause.......................... P.91

Conclusive Argument......................................P.105

**PART III:
The Political Analysis of Amendment
XIV**..P.109

Introductory Argument..................................P.111

Chapter VII:
Citizenship in Democratic Society....................P.113

Chapter VIII:
Birthright Citizenship....................................P.131
and Illegal Immigration

Conclusive Argument......................................P.137

General Conclusion..P.143

Works Cited..P. 153

EQUAL UNDER THE LAW

About The Author

Germinal Gérard Van was born on February 27, 1990, in Abidjan, Cote d'Ivoire (Ivory Coast) in West Africa. He pursued his primary education in Abidjan. In 2001, he and his sister, Jennifer, moved to Nairobi, Kenya, to complete his secondary education. He subsequently returned to Abidjan in 2005 to finish up his secondary education, then earned his High School Diploma in 2010.

He moved to the United States that same year with a student visa to complete his undergraduate education. As he is not a native English speaker, Germinal had to enroll in intensive English classes for non-English native speakers as a prerequisite before embarking on his undergraduate studies at the

A Reflection on Amendment XIV

Catholic University of America. The program was meant to last at most a full academic year. In 2011, Germinal was able to start his undergraduate studies. At the Catholic University of America, Germinal majored in Government(comparative politics) and minored in Philosophy and French Literature. He obtained his BA in Government in 2014.

During the Fall of 2015, Germinal enrolled at the George Washington University to complete an MA in Politics, and graduated in 2017. Debating politics has always been a passion for Germinal. He has therefore decided to convert that passion for politics into writing. He believes that expressing political thoughts into writings is the best way to sensitize and educate those who have been fed by the mass media due to their limited access to education. Germinal has naturally focused his work on politics, especially on political and legal theory. He has published some of his essays on his LinkedIn page and finally wrote his very first book on his thoughts regarding the way whereby politics transcends into the culture in the United States. On April 18, 2018, Germinal authored his first

EQUAL UNDER THE LAW

book titled *American Political Culture: An Observation From The Outside.*

A Reflection on Amendment XIV

EQUAL UNDER THE LAW

Acknowledgments

The list of people that I am showing gratefulness has not shrunk. It has instead extended. Of course, I would like to thank at first my wife and my sister for their unconditional support. Their emotional support was necessary for the implementation of this project.

Furthermore, I would like to thank my very good friend Alex M. Joensen for his intellectual contribution. Alex is an alumni of the Catholic University of America and a graduate of the University of Maryland.

Undoubtedly, it is essential to mention the participation of Professor Mohamed B. Keita into this work. As a distinguished scholar, Dr. Keita provided an extensive proofread to manuscript and suggested ideas that shaped the work. Dr. Mohamed B. Keita is

A Reflection on Amendment XIV

a Professor of Political Science at the George Washington University. He holds a Ph.D. from Howard University. Professor Keita has published several books and articles. His most notable work is his doctoral dissertation which is entitled *The Political History of Cote d'Ivoire From 1936 to 2011: The Politics of Ethnicity, Region, and Religion.*

Finally, I would like to mention John Jaros, the brother of my father-in-law. John Jaros is also an intellectual. He is an alumnus of DePaul University. He holds a Bachelor's Degree in History.

EQUAL UNDER THE LAW

A Reflection on Amendment XIV

EQUAL UNDER THE LAW

The Author's Note

Citizenship is an issue that personally matters to me. It matters to me because it is the fundamental entitlement that defines an individual in a politically organized society. For an individual to enjoy the freedom to fully exercise his political liberties, he ought to be a citizen. In this book, I accentuated my work on the preponderance of the Fourteenth Amendment and the role it plays in the concept of citizenship. I do not hold a law degree, nor that am I a lawyer; but through reading the language of the Fourteenth Amendment, I understood its interpretation.

I decided to write this book because I want to share with the reader the importance of the Fourteenth Amendment in our lives and why it matters to all of us. To born-citizens and to

A Reflection on Amendment XIV

naturalized-citizens in the United States, we are all subjected to the authority of the United States government, and consequently to the subsequent states that legitimize the authority of their jurisdiction. Fourteenth Amendment dictates a set of principles that precludes the arbitrary government's action against an individual. The Fourteenth Amendment matters to us because it limits the power of the government to deprive the citizen of life, liberty and property without due process. It is, thus, important to understand its origins and precepts and the conditions under which it enforces the concept of citizenship.

EQUAL UNDER THE LAW

A Reflection on Amendment XIV

EQUAL UNDER THE LAW

General Introduction

The Fourteenth Amendment is a principle of political and civil liberty granted by the Constitution of the United States, which guarantees equal protection of all citizens of the United States under the law. It is comprised of five sections and encapsulates four major clauses; Citizenship Clause, the Immunity and Privileges Clause, the Due Process Clause, and the Equal Protection Clause. The Fourteenth Amendment is one of the foremost and quintessential rights to the United States Constitution. Its [the 14th Amendment] significance plays a central role in American society and jurisprudence because it has greatly impacted the idea of American citizenship.

A Reflection on Amendment XIV

From 1865, which ensconced the year it was proposed, to 1868, which determined the year that it was passed in Congress, until today, the Fourteenth Amendment has shaped the political culture of the United States and continues to do so. It has stipulated the advancement and the betterment of American society as a whole. At the outset of the new republic, racial and gender inequality were already implemented in the culture of the early days. Within the initial ten amendments which constitute the Bill of Rights, the Constitution was primarily written to enhance the rights of the white propertied male. With the abolition of slavery in 1865 and the rise of the former slaves to the legal status of citizen of the United States, the Fourteenth Amendment has left its imprint upon American society and has since, always promoted equal rights for all individual under the law.

The purpose of this book is to analyze the preponderance of the Fourteenth Amendment, and the role that it has performed for more than 150 years in American political culture. The Fourteenth Amendment has set forth its core philosophy as the

EQUAL UNDER THE LAW

guardian of all constitutional rights that encapsulates the Bill of Rights and the subsequent amendments.

Equal Under The Law: A Reflection on Amendment XIV is divided into three parts. The first part focuses on the historical analysis of the Fourteenth Amendment. It establishes the conditions under which the Fourteenth Amendment came to existence. The second part articulates the legal analysis of the Fourteenth Amendment. Undeniably, this second part accentuates on the legal doctrines that substantiate the Fourteenth Amendment as the epitome of citizenship addressed in the Constitution. The third part of the book encompasses the political theory of the Fourteenth Amendment. It argues the origins of citizenship in democratic societies and also underscores the interpretation of federal immigration laws. The two most important concepts are the right of blood, and the right of soil as both determine the essence of American citizenship.

A Reflection on Amendment XIV

PART I

THE HISTORICAL ANALYSIS OF AMENDMENT XIV

A Reflection on Amendment XIV

EQUAL UNDER THE LAW

Introductory Argument

The Fourteenth Amendment is the constitutional right that determines the precept of citizenship in the United States. None the less, the Fourteenth Amendment has an ancestral history way before the enactment of Thirteenth Amendment and the Civil Rights Act of 1866. Before the enactment of the Fourteenth Amendment, citizenship was drastically attributed to a very small percentage of individuals who were financially settled. These individuals were the white propertied males. Blacks and women were not considered citizens because they were not entitled

A Reflection on Amendment XIV

to the alienable rights that establish the power of the citizen. The first signs of rebellion for equal rights appeared in the 1830s.

Although the Thirteenth Amendment was the principal originator of the Fourteenth Amendment, *The Rights of Colored Men To Suffrage, Citizenship and Trial by Jury* published by William Yates, is considered to be the Magna Carta of citizenship in the United States because it elucidates all the political rights and liberties that the colored man (slaves then African Americans) is empowered to in a politically organized society. The publication was a reflection of what is enunciated in the Fourteenth Amendment such the Due Process Clause, the Equal Protection Clause and the Citizenship Clause. It ascertained the emancipation of the slave to the legal status of citizen in Antebellum America.

The history of citizenship in the United States has been a long battle for inclusion, for equal rights and equality of opportunity. It is a battle that is still pursuing its course and will surely never end. The Fourteenth Amendment as an individual right, has extended the power of the Constitution beyond the Bill of Rights. It has invigorated the power of the citizen against state's government. In this first part, we are going to learn about the historical context in which the Fourteenth Amendment was generated.

A Reflection on Amendment XIV

Chapter I:

The Creation of Amendment XIII

A Reflection on Amendment XIV

The Senatorial Debate

In order to fathom the origins of the Fourteenth Amendment, it is first of all wise to trace its history from the amendment that precedes it. The Thirteenth Amendment distinctly declares *"Neither slavery nor involuntary servitude, except as a punishment for crime whereof the party shall have been duly convicted, shall exist within the United States, or any place subject to their jurisdiction*[1]*".* Indeed, the first section of the Thirteenth Amendment was initially introduced to the Senate Floor of the United States Congress in 1864.

The purpose of the Thirteenth Amendment was to abolish slavery as a legal institution. Notwithstanding, prior to the Civil War, in February

---

[1] US Constitution. Amend. XIII, Sec 1.

EQUAL UNDER THE LAW

1861, Congress had passed a Thirteenth Amendment for an entirely different purpose—to guarantee the legality and perpetuity of slavery in the slave states, rather than to end it[2]. The willingness to retain slavery as a legal institution and maintaining it as the main economic source caused the outbreak of the Civil War in April 1861.

By preserving the Union, it can be argued that Abraham Lincoln was the greatest president in United States history. Abraham Lincoln had comprehended that it was imperative to elevate the slaves to the rank of citizen of the United States in order to end the war. The near end of the Civil War stimulated the debate on the abolition of slavery in the Senate.

The Abolitionist senators devotedly believed that slavery was contrary to human nature. As the Republic of the United States was found upon the values of individual liberties and the precept of natural rights, the Abolitionists held that "all men were equal" and therefore no man shall be induced to slavery and

---

[2] Leidner, Gordon, "The Thirteenth Amendment" *Great American History,* www.greatamericanhistory.net , Article, Web.

A Reflection on Amendment XIV

subjugation. With a Senate Floor dominated by the Republican Party, the Thirteenth Amendment easily passed in a 38 to 6 vote. Nonetheless, for the legislation to become law the required two thirds majority needed to be reached in the House of Representatives to approve the bill. It was on the House Floor that President Lincoln showcased his political genius.

EQUAL UNDER THE LAW

The House of Representatives Debate

The passage of the Thirteenth Amendment in the House of Representatives was one of the most intense constitutional and legislative battles in American history. The late months of 1864 exacerbated the question of the abolition of slavery. President Lincoln took an active role in the proceedings that led to the approval of the legislation.

As a matter of fact, by prohibiting the institution of slavery and by outlawing individual citizens from owning slaves, the legislature in the wake of the Civil War created the first constitutional provision to directly limit the rights and freedoms of

A Reflection on Amendment XIV

American citizens[3]. President Lincoln was determined to make the abolition of slavery a constitutional right strictly attributed to the Republican Party's platform. He [Lincoln] used all his political skills and influence to convince additional Democrats to support the amendment's passage.[4]

President Abraham Lincoln was to exercise a great influence upon the House of Representatives because as President of the United States, he had the ability to expand his prerogative powers during wartime. The majority of Congressmen who were against the passage of the Thirteenth Amendment did so in order to combat the Emancipation Proclamation since it was an executive order issued by President Lincoln in 1863, which freed all slaves held in geographical areas in rebellion against the United States.

---

[3] Perkiss, Abigail, "Abraham Lincoln As Constitutional Radical: The 13th Amendment" *Constitutional Daily,* www.constitutionalcenter.org , Article, Web.
[4] Leidner, Gordon, "The Thirteenth Amendment" *Great American History.* www.greatamericanhistory.net. Article. Web.

EQUAL UNDER THE LAW

The passage of the Thirteenth Amendment in the House would be more strenuous due to the greater power of Democrats, who favored state's rights over federal action, and moderate Republicans who sought peace at any price, even if it meant the perpetuation of slavery. When the House voted on the amendment in June 1864, it only garnered 93 votes, thirteen short of the two-thirds majority required for passage. Only four Democrats broke ranks to vote in the amendment's favor[5].

It is obvious that the Thirteenth Amendment passed with great difficulty in Congress. However, what it demonstrates to us is that it [the 13th Amendment] is a constitutional right that will never be amended because it has entrenched itself as the generator of equal justice and equal protection under the law. The Thirteenth Amendment is the root precept of the Fourteenth Amendment.

---

[5] Klein, Christopher, "Congress Passes 13th Amendment, 150 Years Ago". *History Stories,* Jan 30, 2015. www.history.com. Article. Web

A Reflection on Amendment XIV

Chapter II :

The Fourteenth Amendment and Its Ratification

A Reflection on Amendment XIV

The Proposal of the Fourteenth Amendment

The victorious enactment of the Thirteenth Amendment brought into sharp relief the question of citizenship and the possible need for a clearer definition of said citizenship. The destruction the Civil War wrought introduced the United States into a new era—the Reconstruction Era. Abraham Lincoln's assassination in April 1865 left his successor, Andrew Johnson, to preside over the complex process of incorporating former Confederate states back into the Union after the Civil War and establishing former slaves as free and equal citizens[6].

---

[6] "14th Amendment", *History*, www.history.com

EQUAL UNDER THE LAW

Johnson, a Democrat (and former slaveholder) from Tennessee, supported emancipation, but he differed greatly from Republican-controlled Congress in his views of how the Reconstruction should proceed. President Johnson showed relative leniency toward the former Confederate states as they were reintroduced into the Union[7].

The Fourteenth Amendment was proposed primarily by Ohio lawyer and politician John Bingham. He was the man who enumerated the very first ideas of the Fourteenth Amendment in 1863 because he remarkably anticipated the limitations of the Constitution upon the States in favor of personal liberty of all of the citizens of the Republic[8]. John Bingham took the lead in framing the Fourteenth Amendment and he authored the guarantee that no

---

[7] Ibid.
[8] Magliocca, Gerard N. "The Father of the Fourteenth Amendment", *The New York Times.* Sept 17, 2013. Article. Web.

A Reflection on Amendment XIV

state shall "deny to any person within its jurisdiction the equal protection of the laws"[9].

The Civil Rights Act, passed by Congress in April 1866, would eventually have a great impact on constitutional rights. It was a piece of legislation that encompassed several statutes which aimed at protecting the rights of the newly freed slaves, as many of them were vetoed by President Johnson[10].

One important point to highlight in the Civil Rights Act of 1866 is that it granted legal protection to all individuals born in the United States. Which means that it is the piece of legislation that legally and legitimately substantiated the former slave as a United States citizen. As the spirit of Magna Carta was incorporated into the Bill of Rights, the spirit of the Civil Rights Act of 1866 was also assimilated to the Fourteenth Amendment. The proposal of the Fourteenth Amendment also had a political aim. It was purely a partisan measure, drafted and enacted

---

[9] Ibid.
[10] "Civil Rights Act of 1866", *History of the Federal Judiciary,* Federal Judicial Center. www.fjc.gov. Article.

entirely by Republicans in a Reconstruction Congress wherein the Southern states were denied representation[11]. The Republican Party desired to win the forthcoming elections under the label of "slave liberators". Despite the fact that the Civil Rights Act of 1866 was vetoed by President Andrew Johnson, the Republicans maneuvered to implement the legal precept of the Civil Rights Act of 1866 into the Fourteenth Amendment when it was ratified and enacted in 1868.

---

[11] Colby, Thomas B. "Originalism and the Ratification of the Fourteenth Amendment", *Northwestern University Law Review*. Vol 107, No 4. 2013. Article.

A Reflection on Amendment XIV

The Ratification of the Fourteenth Amendment

The conditions under which the Ratification of the Fourteenth Amendment occurred, were extremely divergent from those of the Constitutional Convention of 1788. Undoubtedly, the end of the Civil War fostered the Ratification of the Fourteenth Amendment.

The victorious outcome of the Republicans subjugated the former Confederate states to military rule. The Confederate states would be kept under military rule, and not allowed back into the Union until each state agreed to ratify the Fourteenth Amendment.

The veto of the Civil Rights Act of 1866 by President Andrew Johnson weakened the Democratic political platform in Congress for southern leaders.

EQUAL UNDER THE LAW

The Republicans controlled the legislative branch [House and Senate], which enabled them [Republicans] to undermine the authority of President Johnson.

Connecticut was the first state to ratify the Fourteenth Amendment on June 30, 1866. During the next two years, twenty-eight states would ratify the amendment, though not without incident[12]. Southern states resisted, but Congress, implacably dominated by the Republicans, required them to ratify the Fourteenth Amendment. As a condition of regaining representation in Congress. On July 9th of 1868 Louisiana and South Carolina voted to ratify the Fourteenth Amendment, making the necessary two-thirds majority[13].

From the legal standpoint, the Ratification of Fourteenth Amendment is illegitimate. The Amendment can, therefore, claim no warrant to democratic legitimacy through original popular

---

[12] Kelly, Martin, "The 14th Amendment Summary", *ThoughtCo*, www.thoughtco.com. Article. Web.
[13] "14th Amendment" *History*. www.history.com. Article. Web.

A Reflection on Amendment XIV

sovereignty[14]. Popular sovereignty encapsulates the free will of all parties into participatory democracy. The forcing of the Southern states to ratify the amendment established the violation of the "free will" ideal of American culture and subsequently thwarted the principle of state's rights.

From the political stance, the Ratification of the Fourteenth Amendment is legitimate. This legitimacy is ingrained in the anticipation of the potential forthcoming rebellion of the freed slaves. Avoiding the rebellion would preserve the social peace and social order of the Union. Former slaves and their descendants faced grave threats as noncitizens. In the decade before the Civil War, free African Americans numbered nearly 500,000, or 1.6 percent of the nation's population. Most had lived in the United States for generations, building families, schools, and churches. Their labor was the engine of prosperity,

---

[14] Colby, Thomas B. "Originalism and the Ratification of the Fourteenth Amendment", *Northwestern University Law Review*. Vol 107, No 4. 2013. Article.

EQUAL UNDER THE LAW

whether on rural farmlands or urban cityscapes[15]. The American political elite fathomed that African Americans would be a force that would drive the whole economy. Because of this fact it would be necessary to incorporate and regualte African Americans as citizens of the United States.)

---

[15] Jones, Martha S. "The 14th Amendment Solved One Citizenship Crisis, But It Created A New One", *The Washington Post.* July, 9, 2017. www.washingtonpost.com Article. Web.

A Reflection on Amendment XIV

Conclusive Argument

The year 1866 was indubitably the most significant year in the history of American constitutional politics. Indeed, the Civil Rights Act of 1866 played a consequential role in the enactment of Fourteenth Amendment because it was the steppingstone that led to its implementation. The Fourteenth Amendment revealed itself as a "rebel right" inasmuch as destabilized the status-quo. At the time, the status-quo was ingrained in the power of the white propertied male. Elevating the freed slave to the status of citizen meant that the power of the white propertied male was at stake. It implied as well, that the freed slave was entitled to the same constitutional rights and protections that was accredited solely to the white propertied male.

EQUAL UNDER THE LAW

The Fourteenth Amendment was not only legislated to become a constitutional right, it was also administered to enhance a political agenda. Whether the Republican Party believed that slavery was a moral issue or a political one, President Abraham Lincoln was determined to attribute the abolition of slavery to the Republican party because he was convinced that the freed slave who became citizen would systematically adhere to the Republican Party, which would represent a political force for the party.

We must not forget that the Fourteenth Amendment was the price to pay for the reunification of the Union. Against this background, it also impeded the principle of the right to self-determination because the right to self-determination is the most fundamental political principle that entrenches the power of popular sovereignty. The way in which the Fourteenth Amendment was enacted, was in fact an encroachment of the legitimacy of state's rights. Comprehensively, the Fourteenth Amendment has empowered a certain class of individuals to enjoy the rights of citizenship in a politically organized society.

A Reflection on Amendment XIV

Conversely, its enactment has also infringed the doctrine free-will and democratic sovereignty.

EQUAL UNDER THE LAW

A Reflection on Amendment XIV

PART II

THE LEGAL ANALYSIS OF AMENDMENT XIV

A Reflection on Amendment XIV

EQUAL UNDER THE LAW

Introductory Argument

The Fourteenth Amendment is composed of five sections. In this analysis, our primary purpose will be to fathom and scrutinize the clauses of the first section that determine the preponderance of the Fourteenth Amendment. We will, of course, rely on the most important Supreme Court cases that have thoroughly shaped American society under this amendment.

We have learned in the first part of the book about the substantial history of the Fourteenth Amendment. A constitutional right that took its form in the blood and battles of the Civil War, and ultimately ended with the assassination of President Lincoln in order to administer freedom and equality for all individuals born or naturalized and residing in the United States. This constitutional right would help administer the freedom and equality for all individuals born or naturalized in the United States. The question

A Reflection on Amendment XIV

of citizenship is a matter that has stimulated civil rights and promulgated the fight for inclusion. Even today the issue of citizenship is not totally solved, yet, it is guaranteed in the Constitution of the United States as a right to all.

Chapter III:

The Citizenship Clause

A Reflection on Amendment XIV

The Concept of the Citizenship Clause of the Fourteenth Amendment

The precept of citizenship is defined in the first section of the Fourteenth Amendment. It avows that, *"all persons born or naturalized in the United States, and subject to the jurisdiction thereof, are citizens of the United States and the States wherein they reside"*[16]. This declaratory phrase established the birthright citizenship as a statutory federal regulation.

The Citizenship Clause has a very egalitarian approach. Indeed, it demonstrates that individuals who were not considered citizens before the Reconstruction Era, such as African Americans, had

---

[16] Us. Const. Amend. XIV, Sec 1.

EQUAL UNDER THE LAW

now the same right as the white propertied man. The only controversy regarding the scope of the Citizenship Clause involves whether children born to unauthorized immigrants are "subject to the jurisdiction" of the United States[17].

The Citizenship Clause takes roots from the Civil Rights Act of 1866. It [Citizenship Clause] constitutionalized and validated the Civil Rights Act because some had questioned whether the Thirteenth Amendment was a sufficient basis for its constitutionality[18]. It codifies the fundamental rights that an individual shall enjoy. None the less, by itself, birth within the territorial limits of the United States, as the case of the Native Americans indicated that it did not make one automatically "subject to the jurisdiction" of the United States[19].

---

[17] Rodriguez, Cristina M. "The Citizenship Clause, Original Meaning and the Egalitarian Unity of the Fourteenth Amendment"(2009). *Faculty Scholarship Series.* 4335.
[18] Erler, Edward " Defining Citizens: Congress, Citizenship, and the Meaning of the Fourteenth Amendment" *The Heritage Foundation.* Feb 17, 2011. www.heritsge.org. Article. Web
[19] Ibid.

A Reflection on Amendment XIV

When we pay attention to the words of the Clause, we understand that the word "jurisdiction" has in fact, a quintessential role in the context. As a matter of fact, the word "jurisdiction" in the Citizenship Clause implied a consensual allegiance of the individual to the state, rather than his unwilling submission to the enforcement of the laws of the territory wherein he resides. The character of the Citizenship Clause changed progressively from its enactment and continues to be interpreted to this day in 2018.

EQUAL UNDER THE LAW

The Judicial Interpretation of the Citizenship Clause

It is unequivocal that of all the political events that have shaped the history of the United States, the Fourteenth Amendment was among the most important ones. Ultimately, this heavy burden would be heard in the Supreme Court of the United States, and become amongst its most substantial decisions in American history. As we have learned in *American Political Culture : An Observation From the Outside,* the Supreme Court split into two antagonistic judicial philosophies; that of Originalism and the Living Constitution theory. Upon the question of birthright rule, the Court is surprisingly not as divided upon its [birthright rule] interpretation.

A Reflection on Amendment XIV

In American jurisprudence, the theory of the birthright rule is subjected to two essential theories which define the substance of the Citizenship Clause. These two theories are *jus sanguinis* and *jus soli*. Even at a quick glance, the Latin roots of these words give us an insight into the meaning of these theories. *Jus sanguinis* elucidates the notion of "law of blood", which determines the fact that an individual is automatically a citizen if his parents are also born citizens of the same country. *Jus soli* epitomizes the "law of soil", which actuates the point that an individual is a citizen if he is born or naturalized in the territory wherein he seeks citizenship. Under the "Law of the Soil" this individual is considered a citizen even his parents are not born in that territory.

The Originalists (the Court's right-wing), are believers in the original intent and meaning of the words of the Constitution. The birthright rule is a puzzling question that ought to be addressed from the extraction of the precept. The notion of "natural born citizen" was likely a term of art derived from the idea of the "natural born subject" in English law[20]. Departing from this concept, we can clearly see that the majority of former slaves who became United States citizens following the enactment of the Fourteenth Amendment, would be considered "natural born subjects".

The concept of "natural born subject" goes back to the legal analysis of Sir Blackstone. Blackstone's understanding derived from the common law, which seems to have originated in Calvin's case, in a decision of a Court of Common Pleas. The concept of allegiance to the sovereign at birth, was then, the fundamental criterion for who was—and was not—a natural born subject. Natural allegiance was based primarily upon being born within the territory subject to the sovereign's rules[21].

The Originalists are more inclined to embrace the concept of the "natural-born subject" of Sir

---

[20] Solum, Lawrence B., "Originalism and the Natural Born Citizen Clause", *Georgetown Law Journal,* Georgetown Law Center. 2007. Article.
[21] Ibid.

A Reflection on Amendment XIV

Blackstone since American jurisprudence has been directly inherited from English jurisprudence. Notwithstanding, the Citizenship Clause also accentuated upon the word "naturalized" as mentioned in section 1 of the Fourteenth Amendment "all persons born or naturalized in the United States…" The word "naturalized" established the main difference between English and American jurisprudence upon the comprehension of citizenship. The semantic of "naturalized" entrenched the precept of *jus soli* (the law of soil). It ["naturalized"]stipulated the principle that an individual is a citizen of the United States if he was born on American soil despite his parents not being born as Americans.

The evolutionary theorists of the Court do not entirely disagree with their originalists counterpart. The liberal wing of the Court is more empathic to the law of soil. The reason is that since the United States is a country of opportunity, underlined by the concept of diversity, the naturalization of an individual in becoming a citizen enables that individual to pledge allegiance to the sovereign—escaping then the "natural born subject" theory.

The birthright rule strengthened the idea of the Fourteenth Amendment because it gives value to the individual. The preponderance of the birthright rule was authenticated in the landmark Supreme Court case *United States v. Wong Kim Ark*. *United States v. Wong Kim Ark* fortified the relevance of the Citizenship Clause because the Supreme Court's decision in that case shaped America's perception and policies on the Citizenship Clause.

To vividly summarize the case, Wong Kim Ark was born in San Francisco, California. He went to visit his parents in China when he was 21 years old. Upon his return to the United States, Wong was denied entry to the United States on the ground that he was not a citizen because the Chinese Exclusion Act denied citizenship to Chinese immigrants[22]. The main question that the Court demanded to know was if the government could deny citizenship to persons born in

---

[22] "United States v. Wong Kim Ark". *Oyez,* May 7, 2018, www.oyez.org/cases/1850-1900 , 169US649

A Reflection on Amendment XIV

the United States in violation of the Fourteenth Amendment[23]. The Court held that a child born in the United States to parents of a foreign decent is a citizen of the United States. The two exceptions being, 1) the parents are foreign diplomats, or 2) the child was born to parents who are nationals of an enemy nation that is engaged in hostile occupation of the country's territory[24]. The Court's decision has promoted the principle of *jus soli* as an equal doctrine as *jus sanguinis*. It was therefore promulgated that the naturalized citizen be entitled and protected by the subsequent amendments of the Bill of Rights, and was added against the arbitrary power of the government (state legislature).

In the recent years, immigration policies have been hardened toward individuals who were born on U.S. soil to unauthorized immigrants. In this context, the Obama's administration has mercilessly deported more unauthorized immigrants than any other

---

[23] Ibid.
[24] Lyon, Cherstin M. "United States v. Wong Kim Ark", *Denso Encyclopedia*. California State University, San Bernardino. Article.

administration in order to regulate immigration law. Obviously, it seems unfair to separate a child from his parent because of a legal status issue. However, in order for the rule of law to be upheld as put forth in the citizenship clause, the child born on US soil and the parent unauthorized alien, must comply to the laws of the jurisdiction wherein they reside. If this is not accomplished, the individual's citizenship can never by wholly legitimized. What this implies is that an unauthorized alien cannot be protected by the Fourteenth Amendment because his allegiance is subjected to a foreign sovereignty.

A Reflection on Amendment XIV

Chapter IV:

The Privileges or Immunities Clause

A Reflection on Amendment XIV

The Concept of the Privileges or Immunities Clause

The second clause of the Fourteenth Amendment to the Constitution of the United States articulates that, "No State shall make or enforce any law which shall abridge the privileges or immunities of the citizens of the United States."[25] This statement asserts that a citizen of the United States is protected by the power of the Bill of Rights against the arbitrary power of the legislature (state and federal government).

The Privileges or Immunities Clause is a significant component of the Fourteenth Amendment because it provides the constitutional right that an individual needs in order fulfill personal and collective

---

[25] US Const. Amend XIV, Sec 1, Clause 2

advancement. The Privileges or Immunities Clause unprecedently originated the precept of popular sovereignty in the United States.

The main point to emphasize in the Privileges or Immunities Clause is that the structure of section 1 of the Fourteenth Amendment gave systematic advantage to citizens over noncitizens.[26] Citizenship is a highly coveted right today, especially for people in the United States that do not have it, or after naturalization, are at risk of losing it[27]. The Privileges and Immunities Clause of the Fourteenth Amendment offers a deep protection against state action to a narrow class of individuals, namely those who enjoy the status of citizenship, as defined in the first sentence of section 1[28]. Citizenship by either laws of England or the United States enables citizens to hold and convey, to inherit, to make and enforce contracts.

---

[26] Richard A. Epstein, "Further Thoughts on the Privileges or Immunities Clause of the Fourteenth Amendment", *New York University Journal of Law and Liberty*. 1096 (2005).
[27] Ibid.
[28] Ibid.

A Reflection on Amendment XIV

and give evidences to be free of any special trade hindrance such as high duties[29].

The Privileges or Immunities Clause was written to require the states to protect the enumerated rights of citizenship, such as those listed in the first eight amendments to the Constitution, along with the natural rights of due process and equal protection[30].

Intrinsically, the Privileges or Immunities Clause reinforced the legitimacy of the concept of citizenship—citizenship is what determines the substance of an individual within a politically organized society. Undeniably, as any citizen is entitled to life, liberty and property, the Privileges or Immunities Clause plays the role of the guardian of these three principles (life, liberty, property). In this sense, it obliviates the legislature not to infringe or dispossess the citizen from those rights.

---

[29] Madison, P.A." Historical Meaning of the 14th Amendment First' Section", www.federalistblog.org. 2010. Article. Web.
[30] Lash, Kurt T. "The Fourteenth Amendment and the Privileges and Immunities of American Citizenship". *Cambridge University Press,* (2014).

EQUAL UNDER THE LAW

The Judicial Interpretation of the Privileges or Immunities Clause

Since 1872, there has not been any major landmark case on the Privileges or Immunities Clause of the Fourteenth Amendment. However, the very case that eternally authenticated the Privileges or Immunities Clause as the legal pillar of the Fourteenth Amendment is the Slaughter-House case.

The Slaughter-House case was argued in January 1872 and reargued in February 1873, and finally decided in April 1873. The State of Louisiana passed a law that restricted slaughterhouse operations in New Orleans to a single corporation. Crescent City Live and the Slaughter-House companies received a

A Reflection on Amendment XIV

charter to run a slaughterhouse downstream. No other areas around the city were permitted for slaughtering animals. A group of butchers argued that they would lose their right to practice their trade and earn a livelihood under the monopoly. They argued that the monopoly violated the Thirteenth Amendment, and abridged privileges or immunities, denied equal protection of the laws, and deprived them of the liberty and property[31].

This case transparently demonstrates that the Fourteenth Amendment is at stake, principally, the violation of the Privileges or Immunities Clause. The Court subsequently interrogated the issue of case based upon the ground to know if the creation of the corporation monopoly violated the Thirteenth Amendment and the Fourteenth Amendment.

Contrastingly to what the butchers expected, the Supreme Court ruled in favor of the corporation. Indeed, the rationale of the Court was grounded upon

---

[31] "Slaughter-House Cases", *Oyez,* 9 May 2018, www.oyez.org/cases/1850-1900/83US36

the fact that the monopoly violated neither the Thirteenth, or the Fourteenth Amendment because these two amendments were passed with the narrow intent to grant full equality to former slaves[32]. Furthermore, the Court believed that the Fourteenth Amendment banned the States from depriving blacks of equal rights; it did not guarantee that all citizens, regardless of race, should receive equal economic privileges by the state[33]. Finally, the Court argued that any rights guaranteed by the Privileges or Immunities Clause were limited to areas controlled by the federal government. It [the Court] held that the butchers bringing suit were not deprived of their property without due process of law because they could still earn a living in the area by slaughtering on the Crescent Company grounds[34].

In the Slaughter-House case, the Supreme Court limited the Privileges or Immunities Clause of the Fourteenth Amendment to an attenuated

---

[32] Ibid.
[33] Ibid.
[34] Ibid.

understanding. Whereas the privileges or Immunities Clause did not have many cases argued in the Supreme Court solely on its basis, there is one other case that ensconced the relevance of the Clause. The case *McDonald v. Chicago,* which was primarily argued the merits of the Second Amendment, also substantiated the quintessence of the Privileges or Immunities Clause of the Fourteenth Amendment. Justice Clarence Thomas agreed with the Court's decision that the Second Amendment protects the right to keep and bear arms from interference by law of the States[35]. Clarence Thomas argued in the case of *McDonald v. Chicago,* that the Second Amendment is protected by the Privileges or Immunities Clause of the Fourteenth Amendment. Justice Thomas stated in his opinion that it [The Privileges or Immunities Clause] was intended to enforce the Bill of Rights against the States[36].

---

[35] Shestokas, David J., "The Fourteenth Amendment's Privileges or Immunities Clause" May 2015. www.shestokas.com. Article. Web.
[36] Ibid.

EQUAL UNDER THE LAW

Through this analysis, we have discerned the role of the Privileges or Immunities Clause. We have perceived that it plays a central role in the Bill of Rights. It set the boundary between the power of the central government and the power of individual liberties. It is probably the constitutional clause that empowers the citizen as a political force in a civil society based upon the accentuation of individual liberties over governmental power.

A Reflection on Amendment XIV

Chapter V:

The Due Process Clause

A Reflection on Amendment XIV

The Concept of the Due Process Clause

The Due Process Clause is a component of the Fifth Amendment and the Fourteenth Amendment to the United States Constitution. It deals with the administration of justice. Thus, the Due Process Clause acts as safeguard from arbitrary denial of life, liberty, or property by the government outside the sanction of law[37]. The Due Process Clause of the Fourteenth Amendment reiterates that *"...nor shall any state deprive any person of life, liberty or property,*

---

[37] Wikipedia Contributors. "Due Process Clause". Wikipedia, the Free Encyclopedia. 10 May. 2018. Web.

EQUAL UNDER THE LAW

without due process of law'[38]. This mighty portion of the first section of the Fourteenth Amendment distinguishably empowers the citizen to obliviate the government to exercise a tyrannical power toward his liberties. The Due Process Clause originated from the Magna Carta. The charter that dictated the promise that the king will rule according to the law instead of his mere will. If the king were to deprive a subject from life, liberty or property, he had to do it according to the legal procedures that would not lead to the deprivation.

To understand the Fourteenth Amendment's Due Process, one must commence with the Fifth Amendment's Due Process, from which the language of the Fourteenth Amendment's provision was drawn nearly verbatims.[39] The American Founding generation likely identified the Fifth Amendment's Due Process Clause with the clauses, prevalent in state constitutions in 1791, that required governmental

---

[38] U.S. Const. Amend XIV, Sec. 1, Clause 3.
[39] Ely Jr, James W. "Due Process Clause". *The Heritage Guide To The Constitution.* www.heritage.org , Article, Web.

A Reflection on Amendment XIV

deprivation's of life, liberty or property to conform to the law of the land[40]. The core meaning of "law of the land" provisions, dating back to the Magna Carta, is to secure the principle of legality by ensuring that executive and judicial deprivations are grounded in valid legal authority[41]. In this respect, the Fifth Amendment's Due Process Clause limits the substance of executive and judicial action by requiring it to be grounded in law[42]. It is in this perspective that the Fourteenth Amendment's Due Process Clause defined its legal precepts. The Due Process Clause of the Fourteenth Amendment is composed of two essential elements. Procedural Due Process and Substantive Due Process.

---

[40] Ibid.
[41] Ibid.
[42] Ibid.

EQUAL UNDER THE LAW

Procedural Due Process

The Procedural Due Process is a legal doctrine which is a component of American jurisprudence and an element of its constitutional law. It articulates the legal principle that the government (state and central) ought to follow fair procedures before depriving the citizen from life, liberty or property.

The Procedural Due Process requires the government to inform the individual being subjected to deprivation, to allow the individual to be heard, and to decide upon the individual's case with a neutral approach. The Procedural Due Process insulates the fundamental rights of the citizen against the subjective power of the government.

The Procedural Due Process encapsulates a set of proceedings (these proceedings are not the definitive procedure within the procedural due process) that are compulsory in order to circumvent unjust deprivation.

A Reflection on Amendment XIV

These proceedings are: (1) an unbiased tribunal, (2) notice of the proposed action and the grounds for said action. (3) opportunity to present the reasons why the proposed action should not be taken, (4) the right to present evidence, (5) the right to know opposing evidence, (6) the right to cross-examine adverse witnesses, (7) a decision based exclusively on the evidence presented, (8) opportunity to be represented by counsel, (9) requirement that the tribunal prepares a record of evidence presented, and (10), requirement that the tribunal prepare written findings of facts and reasons for its decision[43].

---

[43] "Due Process" *Legal Information Institute.* Article originally written by Peter Strauss.

EQUAL UNDER THE LAW

Substantive Due Process

Substantive Due Process is to be distinguished from Procedural Due Process. The distinction arises from the words "of law" in the phrase "due process of law". Procedural Due Process protects individuals against the coercive power of government by ensuring adjudication processes[44]. In contrast, Substantive Due Process protects the individual against majoritarian policy enactments that exceed the limits of government authority[45]. Substantive Due Process spotlights upon the validation of rules and legal principles. It [Substantive Due Process] plays a supplementary role of the Procedural Due Process.

---

[44] Wikipedia Contributors, "Substantive Due Process", *Wikipedia, The Free Encyclopedia,* 14 May, 2018. Web.
[45] Ibid.

A Reflection on Amendment XIV

The Substantive Due Process of the Fourteenth Amendment is mainly applied to state and local governments while of the Substantive Due Process of the Fifth Amendment restrains the power of the central government. According to the legal scholar and Constitutional Law Professor, Professor Erwin Chemerinsky, Substantive Due Process concentrates on whether there is sufficient evidence and reasons that substantively justify such deprivation.

Judicial Interpretation of the Due Process Clause

Tennessee v. Lane is probably the most eminent Supreme Court case that highlighted the doctrine of the Due Process Clause. The case was argued in 2004 and ended with a narrow outcome in favor of the State of Tennessee. In order to fathom the rationale of the Court that led to its decision, let's first review the facts of the case.

George Lane and Beverly Jones were disabled and could not access upper floors in Tennessee state courthouses[46]. Both disabled, they decided to sue the State of Tennessee based upon the grounds that they

---

[46] "Tennessee v. Lane", *Oyez,* 15 May 15, 2018, www.oyez.org/cases/2003/02-1667

A Reflection on Amendment XIV

have been denied public services due to their handicap. According to Title II of the Americans Disabilities Act (ADA) of 1990, no person may be denied access to "services, programs, or activities" on the basis of disability. The Act allows alleged victims of discrimination to sue states for damages[47]. In retaliation to the allegations, the State of Tennessee filed for dismissal on the ground that the U.S. Supreme Court ruled that Congress had acted unconstitutionally in granting citizens the rights to sue states for disability under the Fourteenth Amendment's Equal Protection Clause[48]. However, the district courts rejected the request for dismissal, the case made it to the highest court in the land.

Thereafter reviewing the facts of the case, the Supreme Court attempted to solve the interrogation to know if the ADA violated the sovereign immunity of the Eleventh Amendment based on Congress' Fourteenth Amendment's enforcement powers of the

---

[47] Ibid.
[48] Ibid.

EQUAL UNDER THE LAW

Due Process Clause[49]. The case resulted in a 5-4 majority opinion for the liberal wing of the Court with Justice John Paul Stevens as the principal author of the majority's opinion. The Court held that Congress had sufficiently demonstrated the problems faced by disabled persons who sought to exercise fundamental rights protected by the Due Process Clause of the Fourteenth Amendment[50]. The rationale of the Court's decision was ingrained in the precept of Substantive Due Process. The Court believed that Congress had substantive evidence to deprive the disabled citizen of access to services because it emphasized that remedies required from states were unreasonable[51]. Furthermore, the Court asserted that Congress had the authority under the Fourteenth Amendment to regulate the actions of the states to accomplish that end. Wherefore, the law was constitutional[52].

---

[49] Ibid.
[50] Ibid.
[51] Ibid.
[52] Ibid.

A Reflection on Amendment XIV

Section 5 of the Fourteenth Amendment grants Congress the power to enforce the protections in section 1 of the Fourteenth Amendment, namely Equal Protection and Due Process Clauses[53]. Congress' authority to remedy or prevent unconstitutional discrimination under section 5 includes the authority to proscribe some conduct that is not itself unconstitutional[54]. The Court has said that Congress may enact "reasonably prophylactic legislation" when faced with "difficult and intractable problems, [which] often require powerful remedies"[55].

Within the case, it is essential to pinpoint the constitutional right at issue. Title II of the Americans Disabilities Act enforces not only the guarantees of the Equal Protection Clause by prohibiting irrational discrimination. It safeguards the rights of individuals with disabilities that are based on the Due Process Clause of the Fourteenth Amendment[56].

---

[53] Lex, Frieden, "Tennessee v. Lane: The Legal Issues and the Implications For People with Disabilities." *Policy Briefing Paper*. National Council on Disability.
[54] Ibid.
[55] Ibid.
[56] Ibid.

EQUAL UNDER THE LAW

Discrimination on the basis of disability is subjected to rational basis review[57]. States policies that interfere with fundamentals rights are generally evaluated under a more demanding standard. It implies that the Court has demanded that states provide a more persuasive justification for their policies than simply rational basis[58]. What this ultimately requires is an extensive application of the doctrine of Substantive Due Process in this case.

---

[57] Ibid.
[58] Ibid.

A Reflection on Amendment XIV

Chapter VI:

The Equal Protection Clause

A Reflection on Amendment XIV

The Concept of the Equal Protection Clause

The Equal Protection Clause is the most symbolic component of the precept of citizenship that entrenches the reflection of the Fourteenth Amendment. Indeed, the Equal Protection Clause of the Fourteenth Amendment stresses that *" no state shall deny to any person within its jurisdiction the equal protection of laws"*[59].

The Equal Protection Clause of the Fourteenth Amendment was drafted by Ohio Congressman, John Bingham. Although the Protection Clause was ultimately vetoed by President Johnson, the clause's main purpose was to enforce the injunction of the Civil

---

[59] U.S. Const., Amend XIV. Section 1, Clause 4.

EQUAL UNDER THE LAW

Rights Act of 1866. When we accurately observe the legal doctrines that determine the Fourteenth Amendment, we comprehend that the Equal Protection Clause imposed a strong limitation of the government (legislature) upon the individual. It [the Equal Protection Clause] categorically restricted the power of the state upon the individual. A federal, state, or local government may not be able to discriminate[60]. This [Equal Protection Clause] doctrine implied that the sovereign (the government) is legally mandated to apply equal protection of laws to all citizens of the United States regardless of their background, and therefore abdicated the favoritism for the white propertied male.

Nonetheless, in order to understand the Equal Protection Clause , we must first understand its the legal doctrines that substantiate the clause. The analysis of the Equal Protection Clause of the Fourteenth Amendment is grounded upon two principles. The first principle is ingrained into in the

---

[60] "The Equal Protection Clause". Constitutional Law Reporter— Introduction To Equal Protection.

classification of law that germinates the government's action[61]. The second principle articulates upon the level of scrutiny applied to the classification[62]. It ensconces the validation that the government's action has to meet that a level of scrutiny.

---

[61] Temchenko, Eugene, "Equal Protection Clause-Overview", *Legal Information Institute.* Cornell Law School.
[62] Ibid.

EQUAL UNDER THE LAW

1- The Classification of law under the Equal Protection Clause of the Fourteenth Amendment

In this part of the essay, our focus upon the classification of law and primarily will be accentuated on the action of the federal government. The classification of law under the Equal Protection Clause is called the *Suspect Classification*. The Suspect Classification determines the level of scrutiny, which is enforced by the courts.

In American jurisprudence, a suspect classification is any classification of groups meeting a series of criteria suggesting they are likely the subject of discrimination[63]. These classes receive closer scrutiny by courts when an equal protection claim alleging unconstitutional discrimination is asserted against a law or government's action[64]. The government of the United States has classified the suspect classification

---

[63] Wikipedia Contributors. "Suspect Classification". *Wikipedia, The Free Encyclopedia,* 21 May 2018.
[64] Ibid.

A Reflection on Amendment XIV

under three categories; the Suspect Class, the Quasi-Suspect Class and the Rational Basis. These three categories enhance the level of scrutiny under the Equal Protection Clause of the Fourteenth Amendment.

EQUAL UNDER THE LAW

2- Levels of Scrutiny under the Equal Protection Clause

Not all discrimination can be prohibited. The word "to discriminate" simply means to distinguish or draw a line[65]. The mediating principle of the Equal Protection Clause must be one that prohibits only arbitrary discrimination[66]. It is in this perspective that the level of scrutiny comes into play. American jurisprudence has authenticated three levels of scrutiny. Strict Scrutiny, Intermediate Scrutiny, and Rationale Basis. These three levels are administered by the Supreme Court in deciding if the law has infringed upon the right of an individual under the Fourteenth Amendment[67].

---

[65] Fiss, Owen, M. "Groups and the Equal Protection Clause", *Philosophy and Public Affairs.* 1976.
[66] Ibid.
[67] Pippala, Bhanodia, "Levels of Scrutiny In The Equal Protection Clause". *Odyssey.* 2016. www.theodysseyonline.com , Article. Web.

A Reflection on Amendment XIV

- *Strict Scrutiny*

Strict Scrutiny is a legal doctrine that requires the government to prove that the means chosen to achieve a compelling government objective is narrowed, and designed to avoid violation of the right to equal protection under laws[68]. For a law to pass strict scrutiny, the legislation must have a compelling state interest that is done through the least restrictive means[69]. Even if there is a compelling state interest, the government must prove that the law is the least restrictive way to achieve the interest[70]. Classes that fall under Strict Scrutiny include race, national origin, religion and alienage[71].

---

[68] "Strict Scrutiny", *Legal Dictionary.* Web.
[69] Pippala, Bhanodia, "Levels of Scrutiny In The Equal Protection Clause". *Odyssey.* 2016. www.theodysseyonline.com , Article. Web.
[70] Ibid.
[71] Ibid.

EQUAL UNDER THE LAW

- *Intermediate Scrutiny*

Per contra to Strict Scrutiny, Intermediate Scrutiny is less intense but the procedure intrinsically remains the same. Under Intermediate Scrutiny, the law must have an important state interest (but not necessarily compelling) and must be substantially related to achieving the interest[72]. Gender is a well-known classification that falls under Intermediate Scrutiny protection *(Craig v. Boren)*[73].

- *Rational Basis*

The Rational Basis or the Rational Basis Test is the lowest level of scrutiny in American jurisprudence. It is a legal doctrine that objectifies the legitimacy of the matter. A law must have only a

---

[72] Ibid.
[73] Ibid.

legitimate interest, and the law must rationally undertake that interest[74]. Classifications that fall under this test include mentally challenged people, LGBT, children of illegal aliens[75]. The essential point to comprehend regarding the Rational Basis Test is that, so long as the government shows that the classification theoretically advances any government, the challenge fails[76]. The government must rely upon its practical argument that will judiciously substantiate its action.

---

[74] Ibid.
[75] Ibid.
[76] Temchenko, Eugene, "Equal Protection Clause-Overview", *Legal Information Institute.* Cornell Law School.

EQUAL UNDER THE LAW

The Judicial Interpretation of the Equal Protection Clause of the Fourteenth Amendment

In this essay, the methodical approach of the judicial interpretation of the Equal Protection Clause will be different than the previous ones. The principal reason for this difference is based upon the *Brown v. Board of Education* case. The *Brown* case has been elucidated in *American Political Culture: An Observation From The Outside* in which the legal doctrine of equal protection under the law has been reinforced and reiterated.

Most U.S. Supreme Court cases that deal with the Fourteenth Amendment are mainly engrained into the Equal Protection Clause. *Brown v. Board of Education* did not only change American societal standards, it ascertained the revolution of race relations.

A Reflection on Amendment XIV

Brown v. Board of Education posed the question of whether a doctrine of "separate but equal" was compatible with the Equal Protection Clause, as it has been established by *Plessy v. Ferguson (1896)*[77]. The primary intent of the Equal Protection Clause was to require states to provide the same treatment for whites and freed slaves in regard to the class of personhood and citizenship rights enumerated in the Civil Rights Act of 1866[78]. The clause is not limited to racial classifications, in large part because the framers were also concerned about white Union loyalists who suffered discrimination treatment in the South[79].

Throughout the evolution of the Fourteenth Amendment, the Supreme Court of the United States had used the Equal Protection Clause to promulgate the doctrine "Equal Justice Under The Law". Before the Equal Protection Clause, the Bill of Rights was only limited to the protection of individuals from the

---

[77] Smolin, David, "Equal Protection", *The Heritage Foundation Guide To The Constitution.* www.heritage.org. Article. Web.
[78] Ibid.
[79] Ibid.

EQUAL UNDER THE LAW

federal government[80]. Once the Fourteenth Amendment was enacted, the Constitution was extended to provide protection from State governments[81].

In order to ensure the fair practice of the Equal Protection Clause, the Supreme Court of the United States decided to apply different tests to the State classification and its response to fundamental rights[82]. These tests, as we learned in the previous essay, *The Concept of the Equal Protection Clause of the Fourteenth Amendment,* give authority to the federal Supreme Court to overrule an erratic decision from the State Supreme Court and all other inferior courts.

By strengthening the Equal protection Clause, the United States Supreme Court presents itself as the

---

[80] "Before the Equal Protection Clause, the Bill of Rights was only limited to the protection of individuals from the federal government", "Knowing The Equal Protection Clause", www.constitution.laws.com . Article. Web.

[81] "Once the Fourteenth Amendment was enacted, the Constitution was extended to provide protection from State governments", "Knowing The Equal Protection Clause", www.constitution.laws.com . Article. Web.

[82] "In order to ensure the fair practice [...] fundamental rights", "Knowing The Equal Protection Clause", www.constitution.laws.com . Article. Web.

A Reflection on Amendment XIV

guardian of the freedoms and liberties of all American citizens before the law. The Supreme Court of the United States has the moral and legal duty to uphold the doctrine of the Equal Protection Clause, which enhances the fair treatment of all citizens, regardless of their skin color, gender or religion, under the law. The Equal Protection Clause advances the absolutism of the rule of law.

EQUAL UNDER THE LAW

Conclusive Argument

At the end of this analysis, we comprehended that the Fourteenth Amendment has a deeper legal meaning to citizenship than we thought. The Citizenship Clause, the Privileges or Immunities Clause, the Due Process Clause and the Equal Protection Clause play an active and idiosyncratic role to the Fourteenth Amendment. The four clauses of section 1 of the Fourteenth Amendment nurture the right of the individual to a greater extent.

At first, the Bill of Rights were created to protect the citizen from the power of the central government. Notwithstanding, the notion of citizenship, as a matter of fact, was only restricted to

A Reflection on Amendment XIV

the white propertied man. The enactment of the Fourteenth Amendment metamorphosed the political culture of the United States. The clauses of the first section of the Fourteenth Amendment enlarged the notion of citizenship progressively to blacks during the second part of the nineteenth century, to women during first part of the twentieth century (the right to vote in 1920), and to homosexuals in the twenty-first century (*Obergefell v. Hodges* which legalized same-sex marriage). The evolution of the Fourteenth Amendment demands a constant incorporation of all individuals into society because we ought not to forget that the American society is a "melting pot" culture wherein freedom is the primary right and principle granted to all individuals living on American soil.

EQUAL UNDER THE LAW

A Reflection on Amendment XIV

PART III

THE POLITICAL ANALYSIS OF AMENDMENT XIV

A Reflection on Amendment XIV

EQUAL UNDER THE LAW

Introductory Argument

The third part of this book is focused on the political analysis of the Fourteenth Amendment. Mainly, this analysis accentuates on the concept of citizenship and its origins. Why citizenship is such a paramount word and concept in a politically organized society? What role citizenship plays in seeking equality under the law? Does one become automatically a citizen despite the fact that he or she has parents registered under the status of illegal alien? What does the statutory laws say about federal immigration laws? Can an illegal alien be protected by the Fourteenth Amendment?

This series of interrogations stimulates this critique. None the less, in order to understand the concept of citizenship under the Fourteenth Amendment, it is primarily required to draw a

A Reflection on Amendment XIV

theoretical framework on the origins of citizenship. Citizenship has a broader definition for different societies. The notion of citizenship is not the same for Africans as it could be for Indonesians, and vice-versa. One element that every culture and society can agree upon is that citizenship is a privilege. A privilege that an individual external to that society cannot inherently enjoy.

As our analysis focuses on the Fourteenth Amendment, which is a constitutional right granted by the Constitution of the United States to every American citizen. Therefore, we have no choice but to retrace the theory of citizenship from a western political standpoint, since the United States is a western nation.

Chapter VII:

Citizenship In Democratic Society

A Reflection on Amendment XIV

The Greek Approach to Citizenship

The Ancient Greeks were the first society to bring to light the notion of democracy and citizenship. In this essay that spotlights the Greek approach to citizenship, we are going to narrow our framework upon Aristotle's views on citizenship and so as Plato's.

Aristotle on Citizenship

Aristotle believed that citizenship has a central role to play in the administration of the State since "man is meant to live in a political association". Aristotle had a conservative approach to citizenship. Chiefly, he [Aristotle] was convinced that the middle class citizens are essential to the advancement of the State.

EQUAL UNDER THE LAW

Aristotle's theory of citizenship was that salvation of political society lies in the enthronement of rulers of that salutary middle class, which represents the happy mean between wealth and poverty[83]. Aristotle adamantly believed in the power of the middle class because it maintains the status-quo. In Ancient Greece, citizenship was solely granted to the upper-class, those who possessed properties such as slaves and estates. Aristotle denied citizenship to foreigners, slaves and women[84]. The reason for Aristotle's denial is based upon the lack of intellectual excellence of these individuals (slaves, foreigners, and women) that he considered as sub-humans or properties[85].

Direct democracy was the political regime that dictated Athenian society. Since slaves, foreigners and women lacked the intellectual excellence to acquire political wisdom, they were not able to participate in the Athenian general assembly regarding the decisions

---

[83] Mondal, Puja, "Aristotle's Theory of Citizenship and Slavery". www.yourarticlelibrary.com . Article. Web
[84] Ibid.
[85] Ibid.

A Reflection on Amendment XIV

of administrating the State. For Aristotle, a citizen is originally a propertied man who possesses the necessary intellectual wisdom to decide what is right for the sake of the State.

To acquire citizenship, Aristotle prescribed certain qualities like residence, right of suing and being sued and descent from citizens[86]. Apart from the above qualities, a person should be competent enough to participate in judicial and deliberative functions and also the capacity to rule and being rule[87].

Just as the United states functions under the constitution, many of the ancient Greek city states, most notably Athens, did as well. In a constitutional state, a good citizen should know how to rule as how to obey[88]. This principle designated the first doctrines of the rule of law in a politically organized society. Interestingly, the views of Aristotle on citizenship reflect those of the Founding Founders at the dawn of the Constitutional Convention. The Founding Fathers

---

[86] Ibid.
[87] Ibid.
[88] Ibid.

believed that the good and righteous citizen was the white propertied man. Before the enactment of the Fourteenth Amendment to the Constitution, slaves were purely considered as property and only operated at the pleasure of their master; and women were merely considered as sexual objects with no discerning intellect or rational opinions. Their role was strictly restricted to reproduce and provide motherhood to the children at home.

To sum up, the ideal of citizenship according to Aristotle is a restrictive, traditional, narrow-minded and conservative ideal. It was that same ideal of citizenship that the Framers of the United States Constitution espoused in the late eighteenth century because only the rich and privileged individual could inherently enjoy citizenship. Aristotle, as well as the Framers of the Constitution, took the philosophical stance of Jus sanguinis, or citizenship by birthright by blood and hereditary. They [Aristotle and the Founding Fathers] placed confidence in the precept that an individual who was born into an upper class

A Reflection on Amendment XIV

family is fit to rule due to his inherited intellectual excellence of his predecessors.

EQUAL UNDER THE LAW

Plato on Citizenship

The views of Plato on citizenship do not differ from those of Aristotle. Instead, his [Plato] views are supplementary to those of Aristotle. For Plato, the citizen is the guardian of the political community because he has the power to implement laws that would shape political order.

The citizen must also be attached to the political order, and this is achieved through education[89]. Plato was persuaded that the good citizen must be educated in order to fathom the laws and precepts of society. In the *Republic,* Plato attributed a crucial role to the citizen. The citizen is the epitome of self-governance. He [Plato] believed that the citizen is

---

[89] Coulter, PhD, Michael, "Classical Political Philosophy", *What is Needed in a Citizen: Citizenship and Western Political Philosophy.* P. 2. Article.

A Reflection on Amendment XIV

rational enough to decide for himself. That is why he accentuated the need for education of the citizen.

EQUAL UNDER THE LAW

The Roman Approach To Citizenship

The Roman concept of citizenship represents both a measure of their capacity to govern, and their key contribution to western culture[90]. In the Greek city-state, citizenship was something which cannot be separated from the intimate and varied life of the polis[91]. Although there are some similarities, the Roman conception of citizenship is very different from its Greek forbearers. For the Romans, citizenship was roughly in nature of a contract[92]. It assumed that there was a separation between society and state, between the person with interest on the one hand—*res*

---

[90] Robert L. Bloom, Basil L. Crapster, Harold A. Dunkelberger, "3. Rome: Roman Citizenship" *Section I: Athens, Rome and Jerusalem: Background on Western Civilization.* The Cupola Scholarship at Gettysburg College (1958).
[91] Ibid.
[92] Ibid.

privatae, or private affairs—and the state with its interests on the other hand—*res publica*, or public affairs[93]. Roman citizenship involved the possession of certain rights such as the right to property, the right to engage trade, to marry citizens, and the rights to recourse civil law[94]. What was unique about Roman citizenship is that it is securely vested in the individual and not in a community or a constituency like Greek citizenship. It implies that a Roman citizen remains a Roman citizen although he lives beyond the borders of the Roman state.

Unlike Greek citizenship, which advocated for a strict and restrictive ideal of citizenship, the Romans had a more liberal approach to the notion. In the Roman Republic, slaves, women, and foreigners had some forms of citizenship, notwithstanding the fact that it was a limited citizenship. The purpose of granting some forms of citizenship to slaves, women and foreigners, was to expand the power of the Roman Republic and its foreign policy.

---

[93] Ibid.
[94] Ibid.

EQUAL UNDER THE LAW

In the Roman Republic, the role of the citizen was not to incontrovertibly administer the State, but to artfully pursue happiness through life, liberty and property. In this perspective, we detect a correlation between the concept of Roman citizenship and the perception of American citizenship. This correlation is established in the principle of the Fourteenth Amendment. As we are acquainted of the fact that the Fourteenth Amendment aimed to include and protect all citizens under the law, the Fourteenth Amendment expands the power of citizenship as Roman citizenship expands the power of individual liberties.

The spirit of the Fourteenth Amendment is entrenched in Roman law. Indeed, during the early days of the Republic, the Roman government was established with the primary goal of avoiding the return of a king[95]. Its authority centered on a number of elected magistrates, a Senate and small assemblies[96]. The first Roman law code, ensconced

---

[95] Wasson, Donald, "Roman Citizenship". *Ancient History Encyclopedia,* 27 Jan, 2016. Web. 05 Jun.2018
[96] Ibid.

rules that governed, among other things, the relationship between two classes[97]. The reward of citizenship only meant that an individual lived under the "rule of law" and had vested interest in his government[98]. The freedoms rooted in the Roman law code greatly enforced the individual liberties of the Roman citizens as the Fourteenth Amendment strengthens the individual liberties of the American citizens.

---

[97] Ibid.
[98] Ibid.

The Lockean Approach To Citizenship – Consensual Citizenship

It is extremely important to understand the Greek and Roman approaches to citizenship, as they are the roots from were all western political philosophy grow. As we are centralizing our idea of citizenship, precisely from the American perspective, it is imperative to speak of American citizenship from the standpoint of John Locke. Whenever we are theorizing on American political thought, John Locke's philosophy is ubiquitous since he is the eminent source and foundation of American political philosophy.

A Reflection on Amendment XIV

The general philosophy of Locke on government is based upon the notion of consent. What does consent mean? It means that one accepts to give away something in order to acquire something in return. The groundwork of Locke's philosophy has been that man needs to live in a political community in which he has the extensive power to exercise his freedom under the protection of the government. As he is protected by the government, man is also obligated to pay taxes, and supervene the rules and regulations implemented by the government for the sake of ensuring the stability of civil society. It is under this concept of consent that Locke believed that citizenship was also established.

To Locke, the bonds necessary for a civil society are unnatural, they go against the very self-interest that give rise to a civil society[99]. It implies that for an individual to abide to citizenship, he ought to consent to the authority of the jurisdiction [State] wherein he is residing. In return, the State ought to grant to the

---

[99] Alzate, Elissa B. " From Individual to Citizen: Enhancing the Bonds of Citizenship Through Religion in Locke's Political Theory" *Polity 46, No2* (2014):211-232. Article

individual, the adequate rights he needs in order to fully exercise his freedom in a civil society.

The primary purpose of consensual citizenship is to harmonize and consolidate the covenant between the government and its citizens. To Locke, as long as an individual abides to subject himself to the rules and regulations of the political space wherein he lives, he is therefore entitled to citizenship. Consensual citizenship enhanced the precept of *jus soli* [right of the soil] which is reflected in section 1 of the Fourteenth Amendment to the United States Constitution as the Citizenship Clause. As one does not have the power to choose his family, Locke endorsed the saying that "all children are the children of God", which signifies that a child, who is politically an individual, is systematically a citizen of that political space wherein he was born.

We can conclude from this essay that *Jus Sanguinis* [Right of Blood] and *Jus Soli* [Right of Soil] is philosophically derived from the Greek, Roman and Lockean approaches to citizenship. The Greek conception of citizenship is conservative and

A Reflection on Amendment XIV

traditional. From the thoughts of Aristotle and Plato on the matter, we lucidly witnessed that the Greek approach to citizenship indomitably favored the right of blood. The Greeks believed that a citizen is meant to hold government office and perform administrative duties since he directly decides on the rules and policies adequate for the city-state. To hold such responsibilities, a citizen must possess intellectual excellence, and could only possess such intellectual excellence by having parents who are themselves citizens. To the Greeks, citizenship must be hereditary. Conversely, the Romans had favored the right of soil. The Romans have perceived that granting citizenship to individuals, who fit the eligibility to become citizen, would benefit the political expansion of the Roman Republic. The Romans were the first to base citizenship on individual rights and the principle of life, liberty and property long before John Locke took up his pen. Nonetheless, John Locke provided an extensive framework for the purpose of government and civil society [which include the role and need of citizenship] in modern times, which became the spine

EQUAL UNDER THE LAW

of the Fourteenth Amendment to the Constitution of the United States.

A Reflection on Amendment XIV

Chapter VIII:

Citizenship and U.S. Immigrations Laws

A Reflection on Amendment XIV

Birthright Citizenship and Illegal Immigration

The term "birthright citizenship" has become the core issue of immigration law in the United States. Who has the right to be a citizen? What does it mean to be a citizen of the United States? Are children born on American soil from illegal aliens protected by the Fourteenth Amendment? These interrogations are at the epicenter of this eternal debate amongst constitutional scholars.

The term "birthright citizenship" refers to the current practice of considering children born in the

EQUAL UNDER THE LAW

United States to automatically be given citizenship[100]. According to the Fourteenth Amendment to the Constitution of the United States, ratified in 1868 to ensure citizenship for the newly emancipated African Americans, "all persons, born or naturalized in the United States, and subject to the jurisdiction thereof, are citizens of the United States"[101]. The citizenship Clause clearly inculcates the right of soil for any individual who consensually subjected himself to the jurisdiction of the United States. Withal, some constitutional scholars argue with this interpretation because they believe that the completeness of allegiance ought to be paired[102]. It signifies that the individual born on American soil cannot pledge allegiance to another jurisdiction that is not within the territories of the United States.

The text of the Citizenship Clause plainly guarantees birthright citizenship to the U.S. born

---

[100] Raley, Spencer and O'Brien, Matt, "The Fiscal Year of Illegal Immigration on United States Taxpayers", FAIR, September 27, 2017, www.fairus.org/issue/publications-resources/fiscal-burden-illegal-immigration-united-states-taxpayers
[101] Ibid.
[102] Ibid.

children of all persons subject to the American sovereign and laws[103]. The clause thus covers the vast majority of lawful and unlawful aliens[104]. Undoubtedly, the Fourteenth Amendment denies protection to any individual who is not subjected to the authority of the government of the United States, which includes notably foreign diplomats, and aliens living illegally in the United States.

Although the language of the Fourteenth Amendment is limpid and transpicuous, there is an increasing interest in repealing birthright citizenship for the children of aliens – especially undocumented aliens[105]. According to one recent poll, 49 percent of Americans believe that a child of an illegal alien should not be entitled to the U.S. citizenship[106]. Though, 41 percent disagree. The reality is that repealing birthright citizenship would create a self-perpetuating class that would be excluded from social membership

---

[103] Ho, James C., "Defining 'American': Birthright and the Original Understanding of the 14th Amendment", *The Federalist,* August 25, 2015. Article. Web
[104] Ibid.
[105] Ibid.
[106] Ibid.

EQUAL UNDER THE LAW

for generations[107]. This perpetuation of hereditary disadvantage based on the legal status of one's ancestors would be unprecedented in American immigration law[108]. It would also be contrary to the American sense of fair play that rejects visiting sins of the parents on the children. This type of policy would perpetuate the kind of hereditary disadvantage as practiced in many European countries[109]. Therefore, what is the solution to combat illegal immigration?

The answer, in my modest opinion, is to reform birthright citizenship while applying the Fourteenth Amendment. The Fourteenth Amendment does not need to be repealed in order to fix the problem of birthright citizenship for children of illegal immigrants[110]. It just needs to be understood and applied correctly[111]. Birthright citizenship, as

---

[107] Fix, Michael, "Repealing Birthright Citizenship: The Unintended consequences" *Migration Policy Institute.* August 2015. Commentary.
[108] Ibid.
[109] Ibid.
[110] Eastman, John C. "We Can Apply The 14th Amendment While Also Reforming Birthright Citizenship", *Politics and Policy,* National Review. August 2015. Article. Web.
[111] Ibid.

currently practiced, allows those who continue to owe allegiance to a foreign power, to demand American citizenship for their children, unilaterally and as a result of their illegal conduct[112]. The welcome mat to American citizenship is open to anyone in the world regardless of race or ethnic background, as long as they adhere to the legal rules set out by Congress for immigration to this country[113].

---

[112] Ibid.
[113] Ibid.

EQUAL UNDER THE LAW

Conclusive Argument

The third part of the book offered us a crystal-clear and concise political analysis of the Fourteenth Amendment. Furthermore, the different western philosophical perspectives on citizenship allowed us to acutely fathom the principles and precepts of citizenship in America.

The Greek conception of citizenship is based upon a more traditional philosophy because the citizen plays an active role in the State. In a direct democracy, such as the city-state of Athens, an individual is factually a citizen only if he possesses the required intellectual excellence, which Aristotle believed that it is necessary for the governance of the State. The individuals that strictly qualified as citizens were the propertied males. Similarly, at the enactment of the

A Reflection on Amendment XIV

United States Constitution, it was once again the white propertied males who were entitled to citizenship. It wasn't until the enactment of the Fourteenth Amendment in 1868 that gave the opportunity for all people to become citizens. The traditional conception of citizenship is more selective, more discriminatory, and much more rigorous in its conditions for eligibility. In other words, the traditional conception of citizenship embraced the hereditary belief, which signifies that the right of blood prevails.

    The Roman and Lockean approaches to citizenship are similar because they both entwined a more liberal approach to the concept. Furthermore, Locke's beliefs on citizenship are based upon the Roman approach. The Roman approach on citizenship is less uncompromising than the Greek's. The Romans idealized the freedom of choice of the individual to endorse citizenship if it pleased the latter. It implies that for an individual to become a citizen in the Roman Republic, he must be subjected to the authority of the State of Rome. In exchange, the State of Rome guarantees to protect the rights and freedom of that individual. In fact, it is explicitly the Roman idea of citizenship that inspired Locke to theorize about his views on citizenship. It was ultimately John Locke's approach that generated the philosophy of the Fourteenth Amendment to Constitution. The Roman and Lockean approaches to citizenship are more inclusive and promote diversity. As stated earlier, a direct democracy, such as the Greek city state of Athens, is a conservative and aristocratic society wherein very few individuals can rise to the level of citizen. However, a representative democracy, like the United States or the Roman Republic, advocates a more liberal philosophy. In a representative democracy, the citizen is not obligated to be involved in the state, since he or she has the power to elect a representative or senator who will reflect his (the citizen) will in the legislature. The citizen in a representative democracy plays a more passive role in the State. Nonetheless, he [the citizen] still demonstrates his preponderance when he exercises his right to vote. The liberal conception of citizenship upholds the right to soil as the most righteous and meritocratic belief on the condition of eligibility of

A Reflection on Amendment XIV

citizenship. One thing to clarify is that the United States endorses both, hereditary citizenship (right of blood), and birthright citizenship (right of soil).

However, birthright citizenship has become a recent constitutional issue since the election of then-Senator Obama to the presidency in 2008. Not only did President Obama's "birther" controversy bring the constitutional concept of citizen to the fore, it has also helped shape American immigration laws. Some politicians, judges and constitutional scholars argue the credibility of birthright citizenship for children born of illegal aliens. The Fourteenth Amendment translucently accentuates the point that any individual born or naturalized on American soil, and who subjects himself to the laws and authority of the United States government, is therefore a citizen of the United States. The language of the Fourteenth Amendment could not be more factual and comprehensive on this point. Once an individual (born or naturalized) subjects himself to the jurisdictions of the United States, he is not only entitled to the privileges of citizenship, he is also protected against the arbitrary power of the government (state

EQUAL UNDER THE LAW

government) through the Due Process and Equal Protection clauses.

A Reflection on Amendment XIV

General Conclusion

At the crepuscule of our analysis, we had elaborated on numerous factors that determined the concept of citizenship in America. In the first part of the book, we elucidated the origins of the Fourteenth Amendment. In point of fact, the Fourteenth Amendment was created based upon two motives. The social and the political motives. The social motive was to rise the freed slave to the status of citizen of the United States. Slavery became a constitutional issue because they [the Republicans] understood that sooner rather than later, the freed slaves would have disturb the social order by reclaiming the abolition of slavery. The Republicans believed it was necessary to anticipate on the issue by introducing legislation to commence the abolition's proceedings. The political motive was also for the Republicans to bear the label of "slaves liberators". Lincoln fathomed that abolishing slavery and elevating the slaves to the rank of citizens of the United States would grant the Republican Party the label of the party for inclusion of all individuals living in the United States. The victory of the Unionists on the Civil War granted the Republican Party a significant domination in the Congress in both Floors (House and Senate). The enactment of the Fourteenth Amendment shaped the political culture of the United States. It extended the Bill of Rights and empowered individual liberties against state government. It [the Fourteenth Amendment] crystallized the constitutional politics of the United States.

The second part of the book reiterated the legal principles that enlarge the power of the Fourteenth Amendment. As section 1 being the most important and fundamental section of the Fourteenth Amendment, it is divided in four clauses. The Citizenship Clause articulates on the foundations of citizenship according to the United States Constitution. In chapter 3 *"The Citizenship Clause"*,

EQUAL UNDER THE LAW

we cultivated the difference between *jus sanguinis* and *jus soli*. We have additionally learned that the Fourteenth Amendment is in favor of naturalization, which means that it embraces the right of soil. The Citizenship Clause grants citizenship to any individual born or naturalized, and subjected to the jurisdictions of the United States. It signifies that once that individual has subjected himself to the laws and authority of the United States, he is therefore entitled to life, liberty and property. The Fourteenth Amendment also grants immunities and privileges to the citizen of the United States. The principal function of the Privileges or Immunities Clause was to make the entire Bill of Rights binding to the states[114]. The philosophy of the Privileges or Immunities Clause is generated from the John Locke's views on citizenship. John Locke believed that citizenship is a natural right. He held that the privileges and immunities of national citizenship are the natural rights of property and liberty possessed by free persons upon creation of

---

[114] Massey, Calvin R. "Privilege or Immunities" *Heritage Guide To The Constitution.*

government but never ceded to government[115]. The central idea of the Fourteenth Amendment is concentrated in the Due Process Clause and the Equal Protection Clause. The fundamental intention of the Due Process is to obliviate the government from depriving a citizen of life, liberty and property without fair proceedings under the law. Chapter 5 *"The Due Process Clause"* highlighted the two kinds of Due Process. Procedural Due Process and Substantive Due Process. The explicit divergence between the two notions is that Procedural Due Process entrenches the fair procedures that lead to the deprivation of the citizen. Substantive Due Process focuses on the validation of evidences that justifies the deprivation. Equal Protection Clause is the main clause that essentially advocates for equality and fairness. Indeed, it imposed the fair treatment of all citizens by the government. The classifications of law and the level of scrutiny that solidify the Fourteenth Amendment,

---

[115] Ibid.

demonstrated the rigorous constitutional interpretation of this amendment.

The third part of the book elaborates upon the political analysis of the Fourteenth Amendment. Primarily, we decorticated the origins of citizenship. As we analyzed in depth the origins of citizenship, we understood that the concept of citizenship is rooted mainly in two approaches: the Greek approach and the Roman approach (the Roman Approach is the spirit of Locke's consensual citizenship). On the Greek approach to citizenship, our analysis highlighted the main point that citizenship is grounded in intellectual excellence because the citizen is meant to make governmental decisions for the State. The Greek's philosophy of citizenship is a more restrictive and conservative approach which favors the right of blood over the right of soil. The Roman philosophy of citizenship is a more liberal approach. It emphasizes on individual liberties. Within the Roman philosophy of citizenship, the citizen is not necessarily meant to rule society as a member of the government. His [the citizen] primary purpose is to pursuit happiness under

A Reflection on Amendment XIV

principles of life, liberty and property. The citizen is more free-willed according to Roman view on citizenship. It was repeatedly mentioned that John Locke's philosophy on citizenship is grounded on the Roman's view. However, John Locke has tremendously influenced the concept of citizenship from the American perspective. In American political philosophy, citizenship is a natural right. It encapsulates the premise that any individual born or naturalized on American soil, and who has subjected himself to the authority of the laws of the United States government is therefore a citizen of the United States. The birthright citizenship is the essential component of the Fourteenth Amendment because it is the determining factor in asserting the conditions of citizenship in the United States. The birthright citizenship accentuates the principles of *jus soli* [right of soil] through the words "born" and "naturalized" and "subjected to the jurisdiction" in the Citizenship Clause of the Fourteenth Amendment. It is, therefore, controversial to witness the Republican Party, the party of Lincoln, advocating for the repeal of birthright citizenship. It is that same party that enacted the

EQUAL UNDER THE LAW

Fourteenth Amendment and enlightened citizenship in America. It is now that same party that wants to repeal it. why does the Republican Party of today wants to repeal the birthright citizenship? Only time will tell us the real reasons that motivate the Republican Party to do so. As it was mentioned, the most effective way to combat illegal immigration is not to repeal the Fourteenth Amendment but to simply understand it, and enforcing the law solely according to the legal doctrines declared in section 1 of the Fourteenth Amendment to the Constitution of the United States of America.

A Reflection on Amendment XIV

EQUAL UNDER THE LAW

А Reflection on Amendment XIV

Works Cited

Part I – The Historical Analysis of Amendment XIV

Chapter I: The Creation of Amendment XIII

1. US Constitution. Amend. XIII, Sec 1.
2. Leidner, Gordon, "The Thirteenth Amendment" *Great American History,* www.greatamericanhistory.net , Article, Web.
3. Perkiss, Abigail, "Abraham Lincoln As Constitutional Radical: The 13th Amendment" *Constitutional Daily,* www.constitutionalcenter.org , Article, Web.
4. Leidner, Gordon, "The Thirteenth Amendment" *Great American History.* www.greatamericanhistory.net. Article. Web.

5. Klein, Christopher, "Congress Passes 13th Amendment, 150 Years Ago". *History Stories,* Jan 30, 2015. www.history.com. Article. Web

Chapter II: The Fourteenth Amendment and Its Ratification

6. 14th Amendment", *History*, www.history.com
7. Ibid.
8. Magliocca, Gerard N. "The Father of the Fourteenth Amendment", *The New York Times.* Sept 17, 2013. Article. Web.
9. Ibid.
10. Civil Rights Act of 1866", *History of the Federal Judiciary,* Federal Judicial Center. www.fjc.gov. Article.
11. Colby, Thomas B. "Originalism and the Ratification of the Fourteenth Amendment", *Northwestern University Law Review.* Vol 107, No 4. 2013. Article.
12. Kelly, Martin, "The 14th Amendment Summary", *ThoughtCo,* www.thoughtco.com. Article. Web.

13. "14th Amendment" *History.* www.history.com. Article. Web.
14. Colby, Thomas B. "Originalism and the Ratification of the Fourteenth Amendment", *Northwestern University Law Review.* Vol 107, No 4. 2013. Article.
15. Jones, Martha S. "The 14th Amendment Solved One Citizenship Crisis, But It Created A New One", *The Washington Post.* July, 9, 2017. www.washingtonpost.com Article. Web.

Part II: The Legal Analysis of Amendment XIV

Chapter III: The Citizenship Clause

16. Us. Const. Amend. XIV, Sec 1.
17. Rodriguez, Cristina M. "The Citizenship Clause, Original Meaning and the Egalitarian Unity of the Fourteenth Amendment"(2009). *Faculty Scholarship Series.* 4335.
18. Erler, Edward " Defining Citizens: Congress, Citizenship, and the Meaning of the Fourteenth Amendment" *The Heritage Foundation.* Feb 17, 2011. www.heritsge.org. Article. Web
19. Ibid.
20. Solum, Lawrence B., "Originalism and the Natural Born Citizen Clause", *Georgetown Law Journal,* Georgetown Law Center. 2007. Article.
21. Ibid.

22. "United States v. Wong Kim Ark". *Oyez,* May 7, 2018, www.oyez.org/cases/1850-1900 , 169US649
23. Ibid.
24. Lyon, Cherstin M. "United States v. Wong Kim Ark", *Denso Encyclopedia.* California State University, San Bernardino. Article.

Chapter IV: The Privileges or Immunities Clause

25. US Const. Amend XIV, Sec 1, Clause 2
26. Richard A. Epstein, "Further Thoughts on the Privileges or Immunities Clause of the Fourteenth Amendment", *New York University Journal of Law and Liberty.* 1096 (2005).
27. Ibid.
28. Ibid.
29. Madison, P.A." Historical Meaning of the 14th Amendment First' Section", www.federalistblog.org. 2010. Article. Web.

30. Lash, Kurt T. "The Fourteenth Amendment and the Privileges and Immunities of American Citizenship". *Cambridge University Press,* (2014).
31. "Slaughter-House Cases", *Oyez,* 9 May 2018, www.oyez.org/cases/1850-1900/83US36
32. Ibid.
33. Ibid.
34. Ibid.
35. Shestokas, David J., "The Fourteenth Amendment's Privileges or Immunities Clause" May 2015. www.shestokas.com. Article. Web.
36. Ibid.

Chapter V: The Due Process Clause

37. Wikipedia Contributors. "Due Process Clause". Wikipedia, the Free Encyclopedia. 10 May. 2018. Web.
38. U.S. Const. Amend XIV, Sec. 1, Clause 3.
39. Ely Jr, James W. "Due Process Clause". *The Heritage Guide To The Constitution.* www.heritage.org , Article, Web.
40. Ibid.

41. Ibid.

42. Ibid.

43. "Due Process" *Legal Information Institute.* Article originally written by Peter Strauss.

44. Wikipedia Contributors, "Substantive Due Process", *Wikipedia, The Free Encyclopedia,* 14 May, 2018. Web.

45. Ibid.

46. Tennessee v. Lane", *Oyez,* 15 May 15, 2018, www.oyez.org/cases/2003/02-1667

47. Ibid.

48. Ibid.

49. Ibid.

50. Ibid.

51. Ibid.

52. Ibid.

53. Lex, Frieden, "Tennessee v. Lane: The Legal Issues and the Implications For People with Disabilities." *Policy Briefing Paper.* National Council on Disability.

54. Ibid.

55. Ibid.

56. Ibid.

57. Ibid.

58. Ibid.

Chapter VI: The Equal Protection Clause

59. U.S. Const., Amend XIV. Section 1, Clause 4.

60. "The Equal Protection Clause". Constitutional Law Reporter—Introduction To Equal Protection.

61. Temchenko, Eugene, "Equal Protection Clause-Overview", *Legal Information Institute.* Cornell Law School.

62. Ibid.

63. Wikipedia Contributors. "Suspect Classification". *Wikipedia, The Free Encyclopedia,* 21 May 2018.

64. Ibid.

65. Fiss, Owen, M. "Groups and the Equal Protection Clause", *Philosophy and Public Affairs.* 1976.

66. Ibid.

67. Pippala, Bhanodia, "Levels of Scrutiny In The Equal Protection Clause". *Odyssey.* 2016. www.theodysseyonline.com , Article. Web.

68. "Strict Scrutiny", *Legal Dictionary.* Web.

69. Pippala, Bhanodia, "Levels of Scrutiny In The Equal Protection Clause". *Odyssey.* 2016. www.theodysseyonline.com , Article. Web.

70. Ibid.

71. Ibid.

72. Ibid.

73. Ibid.

74. Ibid.

75. Ibid.

76. Temchenko, Eugene, "Equal Protection Clause-Overview", *Legal Information Institute.* Cornell Law School.

77. Smolin, David, "Equal Protection", *The Heritage Foundation Guide To The Constitution.* www.heritage.org. Article. Web.

78. Ibid.

79. Ibid.

80. "Before the Equal Protection Clause, the Bill of Rights was only limited to the protection of individuals from the federal government", "Knowing The Equal Protection Clause", www.constitution.laws.com . Article. Web.

A Reflection on Amendment XIV

81. "Once the Fourteenth Amendment was enacted, the Constitution was extended to provide protection from State governments", "Knowing The Equal Protection Clause", www.constitution.laws.com . Article. Web.

82. "In order to ensure the fair practice [...] fundamental rights", "Knowing The Equal Protection Clause", www.constitution.laws.com . Article. Web.

Part III: The Political Analysis of Amendment XIV

Chapter VII: Citizenship in a Democratic Society

83. Aristotle, *Nichomachean Ethics*. Aristotle believes that Man are meant to live in a political association, and therefore needs intellectual excellence to rule the state.
84. Mondal, Puja, "Aristotle's Theory of Citizenship and Slavery". www.yourarticlelibrary.com . Article. Web.
85. Ibid.
86. Ibid
87. Ibid.
88. Ibid.
89. Ibid.

90. Coulter, PhD, Michael, "Classical Political Philosophy", *What is Needed in a Citizen: Citizenship and Western Political Philosophy.* P. 2. Article.

91. Robert L. Bloom, Basil L. Crapster, Harold A. Dunkelberger, "3. Rome: Roman Citizenship" *Section I: Athens, Rome and Jerusalem: Background on Western Civilization.* The Cupola Scholarship at Gettysburg College (1958).

92. Ibid.

93. Ibid.

94. Ibid.

95. Ibid.

96. Wasson, Donald, "Roman Citizenship". *Ancient History Encyclopedia,* 27 Jan, 2016. Web. 05 Jun.2018

97. Ibid.

98. Ibid.

99. Ibid.

100. Alzate, Elissa B. " From Individual to Citizen: Enhancing the Bonds of Citizenship Through Religion in Locke's Political Theory" *Polity 46, No2* (2014):211-232. Article

Chapter VIII: Citizenship and U.S. Immigration Laws

101. Raley, Spencer and O'Brien, Matt, "The Fiscal Year of Illegal Immigration on United States Taxpayers", FAIR, September 27, 2017, www.fairus.org/issue/publications-resources/fiscal-burden-illegal-immigration-united-states-taxpayers

102. Ibid.

103. Ibid.

104. Ho, James C., "Defining 'American': Birthright and the Original Understanding of the 14th Amendment", *The Federalist,* August 25, 2015. Article. Web

105. Ibid

106. Ibid.

107. Ibid.

108. Fix, Michael, "Repealing Birthright Citizenship: The Unintended consequences" *Migration Policy Institute.* August 2015. Commentary.

109. Ibid.

110. Ibid.

111. Eastman, John C. "We Can Apply The 14th Amendment While Also Reforming Birthright Citizenship", *Politics and Policy,* National Review. August 2015. Article. Web.

112. Ibid.

113. Ibid.

114. Ibid.

115. Massey, Calvin R. "Privilege or Immunities" *Heritage Guide To The Constitution.* www.heritage.org. Article. Web.

116. Ibid.

EQUAL UNDER THE LAW

A Reflection on Amendment XIV

EQUAL UNDER THE LAW

A Reflection on Amendment XIV